QUESTIONS AND ANSWERS ABOUT

SCIENCE

Contents

Matter

Everything around us is matter. Anything that occupies space and has weight is matter. Matter is made up of atoms and molecules. It takes three main forms: solid, liquid and gas. All matter can change from one of these forms to another.

Quick Q's:

1. What is plasma?

Plasmas are super-hot atoms. A tube light glows because the gas inside the tube gets charged up by the flow of electricity and creates plasma that glows. The Northern Lights are an example of plasma occurring in nature. Stars also have plasma in them.

2. What is a super atom?

When some elements are cooled to a temperature just above absolute zero, the atoms begin to clump together to become one "super atom." Super atoms have only been made in laboratories for fractions of a second.

3. Can I look at an atom?

We cannot look at an atom directly, even through the most powerful optical microscopes, because atoms are much smaller than the wavelengths of light that optical - microscopes detect. A human hair is as wide as one million carbon atoms. However, we can detect the position of an atom on the surface of a solid with an electron microscope, so we know it is there.

Q What does matter look like?

A Matter is found in different forms and shapes. It can be as huge as a mountain or as tiny as gravel. It can be hard like diamond, or as soft as silk. Even water is matter. A cube of ice is the solid state of water. At the melting point of water, or a little over 0 °C, the ice turns into water. If the water is boiled, it turns into steam or gas. When this steam meets a cold surface, like a tile on the kitchen wall, it cools and becomes liquid. Plasma, another form of matter, can be made from a gas.

◀ **Underground water**
A geyser blows steam into the cold air of Iceland. The temperature underground can be so high that the water turns into steam. This steam then expands and looks for ways out of its chamber. When it finds a pipe leading to a hole on the Earth's surface, it gushes out in the form of a geyser. On contact with the cold air outside, the steam cools down and turns back to water again.

Q What are solids?

A Anything that has a shape of its own and occupies space or has volume is a solid. An ice cube is a solid. When it melts into water, it turns into a liquid that has volume but no definite shape. If you pour the liquid into a spoon, it takes the shape of the spoon. If you pour it back into the ice tray, it takes the shape of the ice tray. If the water is heated to a certain temperature, it becomes vapor or gas and has no definite shape or volume. Gas expands to fill any container you put it into.

▲ **All three forms**
The ice cubes (top), the water in a cup (top right) and the vapor in front of the kettle (above) are the three forms in which water can be found—solid, liquid and gas. All three forms are interchangeable, by adding or taking heat energy away from the water. The chemical properties of water remain the same in all states.

▼ **Crystal of carbon atoms**
A diamond is a transparent crystal of carbon atoms. It is one of the many forms in which carbon is found.

Q What is matter made of?

A The tiniest part of all matter is an atom. Several atoms form a molecule. Matter in solid state, like the ice cube, gets its shape because the atoms are packed close and tight. In the liquid state, atoms are more loosely packed. In the gas state, the atoms are even more spread out and have lots of space between them.

Q How does an ice cube become water?

A Adding more energy or taking away energy from a substance changes its form. When you add heat energy to an ice cube, it turns to water. This is a physical change since its shape and state change but the chemical composition, or the atoms and molecules, do not change.

Tiny orbit

Atoms are made up of three parts called electrons, neutrons and protons. The neutrons and protons form the nucleus, or center, of the atom and the electrons move around the nucleus. An electron has a negative electric charge, the proton has a positive electric charge and the neutron is neutral or has no charge. The atomic theory was first developed by John Dalton (below).

Q What are chemical changes?

A Sometimes, adding or taking away energy changes the substance so much that no amount of heating or cooling can turn it back to what it was. This is called a chemical change. When you heat or toast bread, it turns brown and finally gets burned or black. No amount of cooling can turn this brown bread white again because the bread has been through a chemical change.

Q What is a compound?

A All matter is made up of some basic substances called elements. Elements are natural substances. They cannot be made artificially. Oxygen is an element. If two or more elements are combined in such a way that they can be separated again, it is called a mixture. When you combine two or more elements to make something new that cannot be changed, you get a compound. If you heat iron and sulphur, it will form iron sulphide, which is a compound.

◀ **Different shapes**
A liquid does not have a specific shape but takes the shape of the container in which it is poured. This is because the atoms that make up the liquid are freer than they are in solid form, so they move about more and occupy all the space.

▲ **A chemical change**
When you toast a slice of bread, it is a chemical change. The heat leads to chemical reactions in the bread, so that it hardens and changes color.

◀ **Plasma**
This is matter in its plasma state, the fourth state of matter. When gases become very hot, like in these neon tubes, they turn into plasma and start glowing. In this state, electrons and protons move about freely, so that the matter is said to be ionized. Neon lighting is used widely in cities.

Light

Light is a very important part of our lives. Without light we would not be able to see the beautiful world around us, and it wouldn't even exist. Light is essential for life to thrive on this planet. Animals and humans depend on plants for their food. Plants make their own food, but they cannot do so without light.

Quick Q's:

1. What is a light year?

The distance that light travels in a year is called a light year.

2. What color is light?

Light usually appears white, but is made up of various colors of the rainbow: red, orange, yellow, green, blue, indigo, and violet (ROYGBIV).

3. Why does the Sun look like a red disc during sunrise and sunset?

During sunrise and sunset, the sunlight has to travel a much longer distance than during the rest of the day. The scattered blue light is not able to cover this extra distance and therefore does not reach our eyes. The red light reaches us, as the wavelength of red is longer. This helps red light travel further. This is why the Sun appears like a red disc.

4. What do the words "opaque" and "transparent" mean?

Solids are said to be opaque, as they do not allow light to pass through them, while water and glass are transparent as light is able to pass through.

Q How long does it take for sunlight to travel to the Earth?

A Light from the Sun takes about eight minutes to reach us on the Earth. This is because sunlight travels at an incredible speed of about 300,000 kilometers per second (186,000 miles per second). Nothing in this universe travels faster than that!

▲ **Source of light**
Light is actually a form of energy that is produced by both natural and artificial sources. A light source is any object that gives off light. The Sun is the main natural source of light. Artificial sources of light include candles and electric bulbs.

Q Does light always travel in a straight line?

A Light travels in a straight line unless an object is placed in its path. If the object is solid the light bends around the edges of the object, creating a shadow. If you place a mirror in its path, the light hits the surface and gets reflected. If you use a transparent object, the light goes through it, but its direction is altered slightly. This phenomenon is called refraction.

Q Why are we not able to see objects on the other side of a wall?

A We are able to see an object when light bounces off that object and reaches our eyes. However, solid objects like a wall block the light from passing through to the other side. Instead, the light hits the wall and bounces back. Therefore, we are able to see the wall but not the objects on the other side.

◄ **A matter of color**
The color of an object is determined by the color of the light it scatters—an object appears green because it scatters green and absorbs the rest of the colors. A black object is black because it does not scatter any light.

Q Glass is also a solid object, yet how are we able to see through it?

A The molecules of solid matter are usually packed tightly together, and therefore do not allow light to pass through them. In liquids and gases, the molecules move about freely and there is a lot of space between them. That is why light is able to pass through these materials easily. Glass is made by first melting sand, and then cooling it. The substance made has the rigidity of a solid, but still has the free moving molecules of a liquid. So the space between the molecules of glass allows light to pass through, although glass itself is a solid.

Q How are rainbows formed?

A A rainbow is created by the refraction of sunlight by water droplets in the atmosphere. When sunlight passes through a drop of water, it is bent in such a way that the various colors that make up white light are split. Each color is bent at different angles. Red bends the least, while violet is bent the most. It is this phenomenon that we see as a rainbow.

▼ A rainbow of colors
The rainbow is always formed on that portion of the sky that is directly opposite to the Sun. A rainbow is not composed of just seven colors. In fact, it also contains colors like infrared that cannot be seen.

Mirror, mirror!

Light usually bounces straight back when it hits a solid object. We can see the object, but it doesn't reflect anything. However, some objects also absorb a part of the light that falls on them and reflect it. Others reflect all of the light that falls on them. These objects create reflections. Reflections are seen best on mirrors as they have smooth, flat surfaces that reflect light better. When you stand in front of a mirror, the reflected light from it falls on you and therefore you are able to see an image of yourself on the mirror.

Q Why is the sky blue?

A The Earth's atmosphere contains tiny molecules of gas and dust particles. Sunlight entering the atmosphere hits these molecules and dust particles. Colors with longer wavelengths, like red and yellow, can pass through the atmosphere without being scattered by these molecules of gas and dust particles. But the color blue, with its shorter wavelength, is scattered by the gas molecules and the dust in the upper atmosphere. This is why the sky appears blue.

▶ Blue water
Water is actually colorless. However, large amounts of water act like the sky and scatter blue light. This is why seas, lakes, and rivers usually appear blue.

Sound

Sound is a form of energy that is transferred by pressure waves in air or through other materials. These waves can be picked up by the ear, which is how we hear sounds. But there are many sounds around us that our ears do not pick up, and so we do not hear them.

Quick Q's:

1. What is the range of sound that the human ear can catch?

A young human being can hear almost all sounds from 15 Hz to 20,000 Hz. With age, you hear less, and find it difficult to catch higher frequencies. A human voice carries sound at about 60 Hz, but a shout can reach 13,000 Hz. Elephants, dogs and other animals can hear ultrasonic sound that we cannot.

2. How does ultrasonic sound help doctors?

Ultrasonic sound waves help doctors locate and diagnose medical problems, because different tissues reflect sound waves in different ways. Using this method, doctors can also monitor the development of a fetus during pregnancy.

3. How do I speak?

Human beings have vocal chords inside the larynx which produce sound. When air passes through a gap between the chords, these chords vibrate and produce a sound. All animals that can produce a sound have vocal chords, except birds which produce sound through a bony ring, called a syrinx.

Q How does sound move?

A Sound needs a medium like air, water or solids to travel through. When something moves through the air, it disturbs the molecules of gas in the air around it. The air vibrates or moves back and forth. This vibration is heard as sound. The greater the vibration, the louder the sound. Since sound travels in waves, it gets weaker the further it travels. That is why your voice cannot be heard beyond a certain distance. If you put in more energy and shout, the sound waves will be stronger and travel further so that your voice can be heard further. Sound cannot travel through a vacuum, because a vacuum is completely empty, and has no medium with which to carry the sound wave.

Q Can you measure sound?

A Sound is measured in several ways: frequency, wavelength and amplitude. Sound waves vibrate at different rates. These are called frequencies, measured in cycles per second or Hertz (Hz). 1 Hertz = 1 vibration per second. A wavelength measures the length of one cycle. Longer wavelengths have a lower pitch. The lowest tones that a human can catch are about 16 vibrations per second, or 16 Hz. Amplitude measures how loud the sound is. A sound wave of high amplitude will produce a louder sound. It is measured in decibels (Db).

◀ Music to the ears
Music generally conforms to eight notes or an octave. All other sound is noise. Although most of us agree on what music is, there can be disagreements. For example, people beating on pots and pans can create unusual music.

Q Does sound travel as fast as light?

A Sound travels far slower than light. Light travels at 299,337 kilometers per second, (186,000 miles per second) and sound travels at about 340 meters per second (1,116 feet per second). This is why we see lightning before we hear thunder. If you hear a clap of thunder ten seconds after you see a flash of lightning, then the lightning struck 3.6 kilometers (two miles) away.

Q What is an echo?

A Sound waves can be reflected off any reasonably flat surface like a cliff, high wall or mountain. When this surface is neither too near nor too far, a sound made by you hits the surface and comes back to you as an echo. The further the surface is from you, the weaker the echo and the longer it will take for the echo to return. The waves keep bouncing back and forth, getting weaker as they travel, until they lose energy and die out.

▾ **Sonic boom**
When an aircraft flies faster than the speed of sound, it is hitting the sound waves in front before those waves have moved away. So successive sound waves are getting mixed up. This creates the sonic boom.

How the ear hears

When sound energy reaches the outer ear, the eardrum that separates the outer and middle ears transmits this sound inside, where it is converted into nerve signals and sent to the brain. The brain tells us what we hear. We hear our own voice much the way we hear other sounds, and also by bone conduction. The vibration of the voice makes the bones in our skull vibrate. These vibrations are picked up by the inner ear. That is how some people with hearing problems can be helped with a hearing aid that transfers sound vibrations to the skull bones.

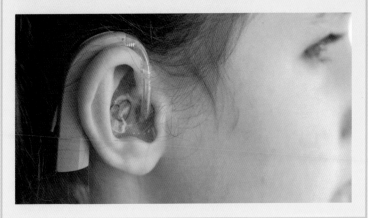

Q How does an aircraft break the sound barrier?

A Supersonic aircraft travel at a speed greater than that of the speed of sound, which is about 1,224 kilometers per hour (765 miles per hour). The first supersonic flight was in 1947 by a Bell X-1 rocket plane flown by Chuck Yeager. These aircraft measure speed in Mach. Mach 1 is the speed of sound. At less than Mach 1, the aircraft is flying at a speed lower than the speed of sound or is subsonic. At Mach 1, it is traveling at the speed of sound or is transonic. Speed between Mach 1 to 5 is supersonic. Above Mach 5 is hypersonic. At supersonic speed and above, an aircraft creates such a strong shock wave that it is heard on the ground as a sonic boom. This can be so loud that most supersonic aircraft fly above Mach 1 only above the ocean, where few people outside will be troubled by the sonic boom.

▲ **Sharp ears**
Dogs can pick up a lower frequency than humans can. Dog whistles are made on this principle.

Heat

Heat is a form of energy that is created by atoms moving. Even things that are cold have some heat energy because their atoms move, albeit slowly. When we feel cold, we jump up and down for warmth to get our atoms moving! Heat energy is also known as thermal energy. Many types of energy like light, chemical, sound, and nuclear can be converted into heat energy by increasing the speed of the atoms in the object producing the energy.

Quick Q's:

1. What is thermodynamics?

Thermodynamics is the study of heat and how it can help us.

2. Why do things expand when heated?

When you heat solids, liquids or gases, they expand because the molecules start moving faster. To move fast, they need more space, so they expand.

3. What is boiling point?

The temperature at which a substance changes from liquid to gas is called its boiling point. The melting point of a substance is the temperature at which it changes from solid to liquid.

4. What are good conductors of heat?

Metals are the best conductors of heat. That is why cooking pans are made of metal to carry the heat from the stove to the pan. Wood and plastic are poor conductors. That is why the handles of cooking utensils are often made of these materials, so we don't burn our hands!

Q Where do we find heat?

A The largest source of heat in nature is the Sun. The Sun is a burning ball of fire whose average surface temperature is 6,000 °C (10,800 °F) about 400 times the average surface temperature on Earth. In the kitchen, we need heat to convert raw food into something that is digested easily. We use gas or an electric oven to heat our food. Before stoves, heaters and ovens running on gas or electricity were developed, the heat for cooking was provided by burning wood or coal. Vehicles like cars move with the heat that comes from burning fossil fuels like petroleum and diesel. Machines like a knife sharpener or an electrical saw generate heat. Our bodies get heat energy from the food we eat. But ultimately, the source of all this heat is the Sun. Even the fires that burn under the Earth's crust produce heat that originally came from the Sun.

◄ From heat to light
The heat energy produced by the burning of the matchstick also produces visible light. The lighted match is used to light the wick of the candle. As the wick catches fire, it produces heat. Some of this heat energy is converted into light energy that we see. Another portion of the heat energy melts the wax to provide fuel, so that the entire process can continue.

Q How is heat measured?

A Heat is measured with a thermometer. A thermometer is a glass tube that ends in a bulb containing mercury. Numbers are written on the tube. The mercury in the bulb heats up when it touches something hot, like the inside of your mouth. As a result, the mercury expands and rises up the tube. If we do not have a fever and are resting, the mercury will stop at 37.0 °C (98.6 °F). When we are unwell and have a fever, the mercury rises further, and the doctor knows how high the fever is.

Q What is heat energy used for?

A We use heat energy every day. Electrical energy is converted into heat energy in appliances like electrical stoves, toasters, hair dryers and light bulbs. When you boil water, heat energy from the stove makes the molecules in the pan move faster. This heats up the pan. This heat from the pan, in turn, makes water molecules inside it move faster and heat up. That is why the water heats up only after the pan is hot. Heat energy does a lot of work for us. The earliest trains ran on thermal power from burning coal.

◄ Using heat
One of the most common uses of heat energy is for cooking food. The heat leads to chemical changes, which turns raw food into cooked food that we can digest.

Q How is heat transferred from one thing to another?

A Heat is transferred by conduction, convection and radiation. Conduction means the transfer of energy from one molecule to the next molecule. Whenever two substances come close to each other, heat flows from the warmer to the cooler substance through conduction. Convection is when a source of heat warms up a liquid or gas due to movements of currents inside the liquid or gas. This is how water boils. Radiation is the transfer of heat in straight lines like the rays of the Sun. Direct radiation from the Sun can be dangerous because it contains ultraviolet rays that damage our skin.

Q How can I light a fire?

A When two things rub against each other, it is called friction. This generates a lot of heat, sometimes enough heat to light a fire without matches. People struck pieces of flint to light a fire before matches were developed. Even today, when you light a match, it is friction that causes the matchstick to catch fire.

▼ Transfer of heat in a microwave oven
Microwave radiation passes through the food inside this oven. Some molecules in the food absorb energy from the microwave beam and start moving around. This movement produces heat that cooks the food.

The largest source of heat energy

Heat energy from the Sun is known as solar energy. Rays from the Sun heat the surface of the Earth, the oceans and the air above. Taking a hint from the Sun's natural heating capacity, scientists have made solar cells from which we can get electricity. When sunlight touches a solar cell, it causes a chemical reaction and electricity is generated. Solar panels can heat water and cook food and solar cells can even run a car. Fossils fuels like petroleum have to be mined from the Earth, and one day we will use them all up. But solar power will not run out for millions of years.

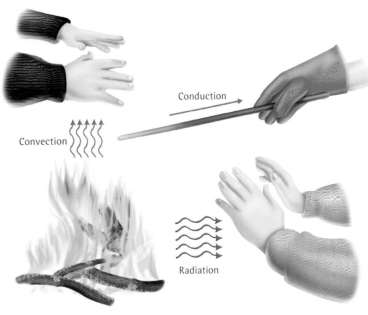

Conduction

Convection

Radiation

▲ Ways of heat transfer
Heat travels through solids by conduction. Most metals are good conductors of heat, while wood is a poor conductor. That is why frying pans are made of metal, but often have a wooden handle. As the diagram shows, convection currents first move upward. Heat transfer by radiation takes place in all directions.

Electricity

Electricity is a secondary source of energy. We have to generate electricity from primary sources of energy like moving water, nuclear power, coal, or natural gas. It can be converted into other forms of energy like light or heat. Electricity is used for lighting and heating or cooling our homes. It runs machines to wash clothes and dishes and to cook. It brings us information through computers and television.

▲ Electric animal
One of the large electric eels of South America can deliver a shock powerful enough to kill a human.

Quick Q's:

1. If electricity lights a bulb, does it also light my torch?

A bulb is lit with electricity from a power generator. Another source of electricity is the battery. It has chemicals that react and produce a small amount of electricity, enough for a torch.

2. How do power stations generate so much electricity?

Power stations convert the kinetic energy of moving water (hydroelectricity), heat produced by burning coal (thermal electricity) or by a nuclear reaction (nuclear power), the kinetic energy of wind that turns a windmill, tide movements (tidal power) or heat from inside the Earth (geothermal power) to generate electricity.

Q Who discovered electricity?

A Ancient Greeks knew that electricity could be produced by rubbing two pieces of felt together. But the first use of the word electricity was by Sir Thomas Browne in his 1646 book *Pseudodoxia Epidemica* (Vulgar Errors). In 1752, Benjamin Franklin proved that lightning was created by electric charges. He tied an iron key to a kite string during a storm and showed that the lightning hit the key. For this reason, Franklin is said to have discovered electricity. Today, we know that lightning is the most commonly seen form of natural electricity. It is caused by clouds carrying a negative charge that bump into positively charged objects on Earth.

◄ Father of the battery
Alessandro Volta was an eighteenth-century scientist who developed the voltaic pile. This was later developed into a battery. The measure of strength of current, voltage, is named after him.

Q What is electricity?

A Everything is made of atoms. At the center of an atom is the nucleus made of protons and neutrons. An atom also has tiny electrons which spin around the nucleus. Electrons have a negative electrical charge, and protons have a positive charge. The electrons don't stay in one place. They move around to different atoms, so some atoms have more protons, some have more electrons. An atom with more protons is positively charged. One with more electrons is negatively charged. When the electrons pass from one atom to the next, it creates an electric current.

Q Can electricity make my hair stand on end ?

A Static electricity is created when you rub against a charged surface. The extra electrons move from your body or the other way around, and a tiny spark of electricity is created. Static makes dry hair stand on end after you run a plastic comb through it.

◄ Natural electricity
The lightning that transfers electrons from negatively charged clouds to positively charged substances on the surface of the Earth is the biggest source of natural electricity we know of. Lightning can be dangerous to someone caught outdoors. Anyone caught outdoors during a thunderstorm should keep as low as possible.

Q How is electricity measured?

A Voltage is the measure of the strength of an electric current. The unit for measuring voltage is the volt. A voltameter tells us how many electrons are sent from one end of the circuit and how many are received at the other end. The distance electricity travels affects its quality, especially if it is prevented from flowing freely because of resistance. Resistance is a material's opposition to the flow of electric current through it. Resistance is measured in ohms. Scientists are always looking for materials like copper that are good conductors of electricity and have a low resistance. Silver is the best conductor, but it cannot be used in wires in our homes because it is too costly. Most metals are good conductors.

Q How does a light bulb work?

A The electric bulb is made of transparent or translucent glass and has a delicate wire called a filament. It has to be thin so that its atoms collide more often when an electric current is passed through it. That is how it glows. Thomas Alva Edison made the first practical, workable bulb for home use. Compact fluorescent lamps that use less energy than other bulbs have become increasingly popular since the 1980s.

▶ Inside a bulb
Scientists experimented with the conversion of electrical energy to light throughout the nineteeenth century. In 1801, Humphry Davy made platinum strips glow by passing an electric current through them. Seven different types of light bulbs were patented in that century before the first could be used at home.

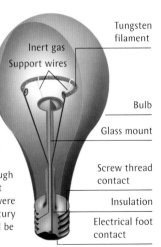

Tungsten filament

Inert gas

Support wires

Bulb

Glass mount

Screw thread contact

Insulation

Electrical foot contact

Electric brain

Without electricity, we wouldn't be able to feel anything! The human body has a continuous flow of electric current through our nerve cells. That is how the nerve cells convey messages to the brain, and we know that our back is hurting, or that someone is standing on our foot. In its turn, the brain uses these tiny electric currents to send commands to the rest of our body. Your hand turns the page when the brain commands it to do so.

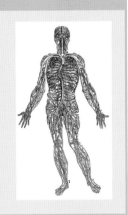

▲ Changing skyline
The night skyline of almost every city in the world has changed dramatically in the last 100 years or so, after electricity came into widespread use for lighting.

▼ A hydroelectric power station
Water is held in a dam. Then a bit of the water is allowed to run through a channel, turning the blades of a turbine connected to a generator.

Magnets

Any object that attracts metals like iron, cobalt, nickel, or steel to itself is a magnet. A magnet can push away or repel other magnets. Some magnets, like iron, are very strong, while other magnets are much weaker.

Quick Q's:

1. Why do things stick only to the poles of the magnet?

Magnets are strongest at their poles so objects stick to one of the poles most easily.

2. How can you destroy a magnet?

Though magnets can be natural or man-made, dropping, heating or hammering them can destroy them, especially if they are small and weak.

3. Can you store a magnet?

Magnets get weaker with time. The best way to store them is to keep them in pairs with the unlike poles next to each other and placing keepers, or pieces of soft iron, across the ends. The keepers become temporary magnets themselves and keep the magnetic force stronger.

4. What is an electromagnet?

Winding an electric wire around a piece of iron can make electromagnets. When electric current runs through the wire, a magnetic field is created. The iron piece picks this up and becomes a magnet.

Q How did people find out about magnets?

A The magnet was discovered in China as early as 200 BC. Around the same time, the Chinese found that from a magnet, one could find out directions like north and south. Sailors in most civilizations began to use a certain type of magnet called a lodestone to navigate. It is the most magnetic substance on Earth. In the sixteenth century, Sir William Gilbert discovered that a piece of iron could acquire the properties of a lodestone if you rubbed it with a lodestone. That allowed scientists to create many more magnets. People were no longer dependent on the few natural lodestones they could find. Today, magnets are made of a blend of different materials that contain some or all of iron, nickel, copper, cobalt and aluminium.

Q What are poles of a magnet?

A Just as the Earth has two poles—the North and the South Poles, a magnet also has two poles. It is easiest to find the two poles of a bar magnet where the poles at either end are equally strong. The north-seeking pole of the bar magnet points toward the Earth's North Pole. The other end points toward the South Pole. But if you use the magnet for navigation, you must remember that the magnetic poles of the Earth are not in exactly the same positions as the geographic poles of the Earth. Also, if you hold two bar magnets next to each other the poles will not point in the same direction because the magnets interfere with each other. The like poles repel each other while the unlike poles attract each other.

▲ **Magnetic scientist**
Michael Faraday (1791-1867), an English scientist, led the study of electromagnetism. He showed that magnetism could affect rays of light.

Q What is a magnetic field?

A The area around a permanent magnet has a force that can affect other magnets or magnetic materials that come near it. This area is called a magnetic field. Even the Earth has a magnetic field. It is like a huge bar magnet. Even if you cut a huge bar magnet into tiny pieces, each piece is still a magnet with its own small magnetic field.

▲ **Fridge magnets**
Most of us are familiar with the pretty and useful magnets we stick on the refrigerator.

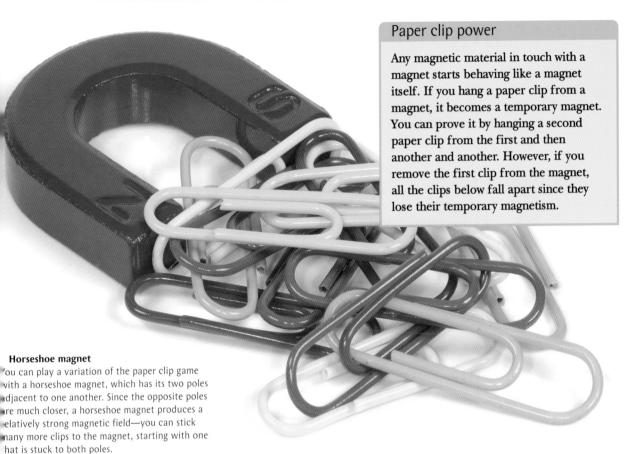

Paper clip power

Any magnetic material in touch with a magnet starts behaving like a magnet itself. If you hang a paper clip from a magnet, it becomes a temporary magnet. You can prove it by hanging a second paper clip from the first and then another and another. However, if you remove the first clip from the magnet, all the clips below fall apart since they lose their temporary magnetism.

Horseshoe magnet
You can play a variation of the paper clip game with a horseshoe magnet, which has its two poles adjacent to one another. Since the opposite poles are much closer, a horseshoe magnet produces a relatively strong magnetic field—you can stick many more clips to the magnet, starting with one that is stuck to both poles.

Q Are mariners the only people who need magnets for their work?

A Magnets are used almost everywhere in modern life. Most electrical appliances, from power stations to the little hair dryer at home, use a magnet to convert electrical energy into mechanical energy. Cassettes are coated with magnetic material that allows sound to be recorded on its surface. Credit cards have magnetic strips that contain encrypted information and enable us to use them. Motors found in dishwashers, fans, washing machines, refrigerators, CD, DVD, and audio players use magnets. Magnets are also used to hold false teeth in place. And they help you remember too—by holding your notes to the refrigerator!

This way is North

◀ **The compass**
Even a small pocket compass can show you the exact direction in which you are traveling. Remember that it is not the point marked North but the needle that is always pointing to the magnetic North Pole. In some compasses you can rotate the dial and align it with the needle to help you find which way is true north. The Earth's magnetic poles shift periodically. The needle points to the current pole.

Forces and Motion

Force can change the state of an object. If an object is stationary, force can get it to move. Once it is moving, force can make the object accelerate or pick up speed. It can also stop a moving object. A stationary object cannot move without force, nor can a moving object stop without force.

Quick Q's:

1. What is net force?

When more than one force acts on an object, the total of all forces acting on that object is called the net force. When more than one force acts on an object in the same direction, the object moves faster. If the forces act in opposing directions, they cancel each other out to a certain extent.

2. What is lateral deflection?

It is a force that makes a bullet spin to one side, or a football curl through the air. During the Soccer World Cup in France in 1998, Brazilian Roberto Carlos scored a free kick with a perfect lateral deflection. He kicked the ball to the far right of the defenders and made it suddenly curve round and zoom into the goal.

Q Where is force used?

A Force is used in all our activities from brushing our teeth to walking, lifting and writing. Every one of our actions requires some force. You need energy to create force. Machines use force to move something or to build something.

Q What is inertia?

A An object tends to carry on doing the same thing, whether it is at rest or moving, unless a force acts on it to change that. This is called inertia. Your pencil box lies on the table until you push it. This state of rest is called inertia of rest. Then, with the force of your finger, it moves on until it meets another force that stops it. This movement is called inertia of motion. If the force you push the object with is too much, it will go beyond the point where you wanted it to go.

Q What is gravitational force?

A Gravity is the force that Sir Isaac Newton discovered, as he watched an apple fall off a tree onto the ground. It is a force that draws everything in the Earth's atmosphere and beyond toward the center of the Earth and it keeps us on the ground. Gravity does not just act on the Earth; it is the force of attraction between all bodies (things) in the universe.

◀ **The science of a kick**
The force of the kick makes the ball move. The force used by someone else's foot makes it stop.

▲ **The discoverer of gravity**
Sir Isaac Newton (1643–1727) is supposed to have discovered gravity after seeing an apple fall from a tree.

As bodies get closer together, the force of gravity gets stronger, and as they move apart, gravity gets weaker. Bigger, heavier bodies are affected more by gravitational force. They also exert a greater force of gravity themselves. Gravity holds the solar system together and keeps the Earth close enough to the Sun for us to get the warmth we need.

Q How do I stay on a merry-go-round without flying off?

A You stay on a merry-go-round because of centripetal force. When you feel you are going to fly off into the air, it is because your body wants to keep moving in the same direction all the time. This feeling is the inertia of motion. But the centripetal force keeps attracting you to the center of the merry-go-round, making sure you stay on board! Objects set in motion normally move in a straight line because of inertia of motion, unless some other force acts upon them and changes their path. When a ball tied to a piece of string is swung round, the centripetal force acts upon the ball, attracting it to the center of the circle. The centripetal force from the string pulls the ball to keep it on its circular path.

Q What is the difference between speed and velocity?

A Speed is the distance traveled by an object in a particular time. Velocity is speed in a particular direction. Suppose you sat in a train that was moving eastward at 60 kilometers per hour (37 miles per hour). You would say that the speed of the train was 60 kilometers per hour (37 miles per hour), while its velocity was 60 kilometers per hour (37 miles per hour) east.

Q What is friction?

A Friction is a force that opposes the movement of an object by acting on it in the opposite direction. The force of friction comes into effect when two surfaces are in contact, and force is applied to make one or both of the surfaces move. Suppose you roll a ball on the floor. The ball will come to a halt after traveling a certain distance, even if it has hit nothing or no one has stopped it. The ball stops because the friction exerted by the floor acts against the motion of the ball. The soles of your new shoes probably have cuts in them to make an uneven surface.

Torque

The force that causes rotation is called torque. Torque can be measured in opening or closing a door, and it is applied when you turn a racquet from side to side. An archer applies torque to move the bow to one side when aiming an arrow. Ideally, the archer should hold the bow loose enough so that when the arrow is released, it shoots straight ahead. If the archer applies unnecessary pressure, the bow will twist upon release, the arrow will not fly straight, and the shot will miss the bull's eye.

When you run, the uneven surfaces of the shoes and the road rub against each other. This friction makes sure you do not slip while you are running. Lack of friction also causes us to slip on a wet floor since the water makes the floor smooth, which means friction is reduced. Friction produces heat. That is why when you rub a matchstick against a matchbox, sparks fly.

▼ Sitting pretty
We stay on the merry-go-around instead of flying off in one direction because of the centripetal force that holds us to its center. The force that wants to make us fly off is called the centrifugal force.

ARCTURUS

This edition published in 2012 by Arcturus Publishing Limited
26/27 Bickels Yard, 151-153 Bermondsey Street,
London SE1 3HA

ISBN: 978-1-84858-161-6
CH002011US
Supplier 15, Date 0112, Print run 1708

Designers: Q2A India and Jane Hawkins
Editors: Ella Fern, Fiona Tulloch and Alex Woolf

Printed in China